ISAAC ASIMOV'S NEW LIBRARY OF THE UNIVERSE

A DOUBLE PLANET?
PLUTO AND CHARON

BY ISAAC ASIMOV
WITH REVISIONS AND UPDATING BY GREG WALZ-CHOJNACKI

Gareth Stevens Publishing
MILWAUKEE

For a free color catalog describing Gareth Stevens' list of high-quality books, call 1-800-542-2595 (USA) or 1-800-461-9120 (Canada). Gareth Stevens' Fax: (414) 225-0377.

Library of Congress Cataloging-in-Publication Data

Asimov, Isaac.
  A double planet? Pluto and Charon / by Isaac Asimov; with
revisions and updating by Greg Walz-Chojnacki.
      p. cm. — (Isaac Asimov's New library of the universe)
  Rev. ed. of: Pluto: a double planet?. 1990.
  Includes index.
  Summary: Discusses the smallest, most distant, and most mysterious
planet in our solar system, its discovery, its peculiar orbit, and its
recently discovered satellite.
  ISBN 0-8368-1232-8
  1. Pluto (Planet)—Juvenile literature. 2. Charon (Satellite)—Juvenile
literature. [1. Pluto (Planet) 2. Charon (Satellite)] I. Asimov, Isaac.
Pluto: a double planet?. II. Walz-Chojnacki, Greg, 1954-. III. Title.
IV. Series: Asimov, Isaac. New library of the universe.
QB701.A85 1996
523.4'82—dc20   95-40350

This edition first published in 1996 by
Gareth Stevens Publishing
1555 North RiverCenter Drive, Suite 201
Milwaukee, Wisconsin 53212, USA

Project editor: Barbara J. Behm
Design adaptation: Helene Feider
Editorial assistant: Diane Laska
Production director: Teresa Mahsem
Picture research: Matthew Groshek and Diane Laska

Printed in the United States of America

1 2 3 4 5 6 7 8 9 99 98 97 96

To bring this classic of young people's information up to date, the editors at Gareth Stevens Publishing have selected two noted science authors, Greg Walz-Chojnacki and Francis Reddy. Walz-Chojnacki and Reddy coauthored the recent book *Celestial Delights: The Best Astronomical Events Through 2001.*

Walz-Chojnacki is also the author of the book *Comet: The Story Behind Halley's Comet* and various articles about the space program. He was an editor of *Odyssey*, an astronomy and space technology magazine for young people, for eleven years.

Reddy is the author of nine books, including *Halley's Comet, Children's Atlas of the Universe, Children's Atlas of Earth Through Time,* and *Children's Atlas of Native Americans,* plus numerous articles. He was an editor of *Astronomy* magazine for several years.

CONTENTS

We live in an enormously large place – the Universe. It's just in the last fifty-five years or so that we've found out how large it probably is. It's only natural that we would want to understand the place in which we live, so scientists have developed instruments – such as radio telescopes, satellites, probes, and many more – that have told us far more about the Universe than could possibly be imagined.

We have seen planets up close. We have learned about quasars and pulsars, black holes, and supernovas. We have gathered amazing data about how the Universe may have come into being and how it may end. Nothing could be more astonishing.

The most distant, the smallest, and the coldest known planet in our Solar System is Pluto. Pluto was not discovered until 1930, and its companion, Charon, was discovered in 1978. Pluto is the most mysterious of all the planets and the hardest to reach. But with improved technology, particularly the Hubble Space Telescope, the mysteries of Pluto and Charon are being uncovered.

Isaac Asimov

Distant and Undiscovered

Each day, scientists learn a great deal more about our Solar System. As recently as the 1920s, scientists believed the two farthest known planets were Uranus and Neptune.

Astronomers could determine some facts about Uranus and Neptune, such as planetary orbits around the Sun. But even when astronomers considered the gravitational pull of every known planet, they could not completely explain the unusual wobbly motions of Uranus and Neptune. Could there be an undiscovered planet farther out that was pulling on Uranus and Neptune?

Astronomers watched the sky to see if they could find a new, distant planet.

Opposite: Like dancers in a celestial ballet, the planets circle our Sun, held in orbit by the Sun's gravitational pull. The gravity of each planet also adds a tiny pull to every other planet.

Right: This historic drawing depicts what is known as an orrery, a mechanical model of the Solar System. This orrery does not contain Neptune and Pluto because they were not yet discovered.

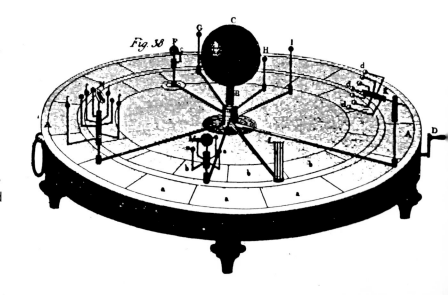

Pluto Appears!

In Arizona in 1894, an astronomer, Percival Lowell, built the Lowell Observatory. There, he searched for a possible new planet. He calculated where it ought to be to create a pull on Uranus and Neptune, but he did not find it in his lifetime.

After Lowell's death in 1916, an astronomer named Clyde Tombaugh continued the mission at Lowell Observatory. Tombaugh took photographs of particular parts of the sky on different nights. He used a device that showed first one photo and then another in rapid succession. With this method, the stars would not appear to move, but a planet would.

On February 18, 1930, Tombaugh came up with a pair of photographs in which a dot moved. The moving "dot" was Pluto.

Opposite, top: Astronomer Clyde Tombaugh found Pluto in 1930 after viewing hundreds of photographs.

Opposite, bottom, left and right: The first photos of Pluto. These pictures, taken one week apart, show that one dot *(see arrow)* has moved – the planet Pluto.

Below: Pluto, the Greek and Roman god of the underworld.

! Name that planet!

Most celestial bodies are named for characters in Greek and Roman myths. When Pluto was discovered, an eleven-year-old English schoolgirl, Venetia Burney, stated that the new planet was so far from the Sun it must get only dim light – so it should be named for Pluto, the god of the underworld. The suggestion was accepted by scientists. As an added bonus, the first two letters, PL, memorialize Percival Lowell, who built the observatory from where Pluto was detected.

Coming Full Circle

As the farthest known planet, Pluto is nearly 3.7 billion miles (5.9 billion kilometers) from the Sun, on the average. This is about forty times as far from the Sun as Earth is. This means that Pluto has to travel along an orbit forty times as long as Earth's to make one complete circle around the Sun.

At Pluto's great distance, the Sun's gravity is so weak that Pluto travels only one-sixth as fast around the Sun as Earth does. And because of its long orbit and slow speed, Pluto takes 248 Earth-years to make one circle around the Sun!

Not until the year 2178 will Pluto finally be back at the place in the sky where it was discovered in 1930.

Left: Pluto is made of rock with a thick coating of ice. The thin outer layer consists of frozen methane.

Below: Pluto travels a longer path around the Sun than any other planet, and it also moves more slowly. The shaded areas show that, since 1930, Neptune *(the inner orbit)* has moved one-third of its way around the Sun. Pluto *(the outer orbit)* has moved less than one-fourth its way.

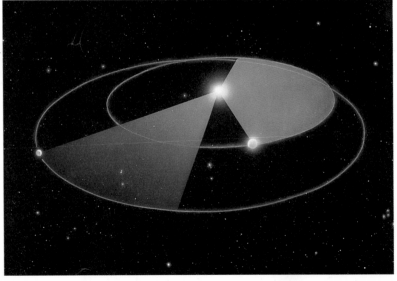

Lopsided Travels

The planets do not travel around the Sun in perfect circles, but in slightly lopsided (egg-shaped) orbits. These types of orbits are called elliptical. A planet in an elliptical orbit is a little closer to the Sun at one end of its orbit than at the other.

Pluto's orbit is quite lopsided. At the farthest, it is about 4.6 billion miles (7.4 billion km) from the Sun. At the closest, it is only 2.7 billion miles (4.4 billion km) from the Sun. This is actually a little closer to the Sun than Neptune is. Pluto and Neptune will not collide because Pluto's orbit is tilted, and it moves under Neptune's orbit. The two planets never come within 235 million miles (378 million km) of each other.

? *The origins of Pluto – a cosmic escapee?*

Could Pluto once have been a moon of Neptune? It's no bigger than a middle-sized moon, and due to its lopsided orbit, it moves in closer to the Sun than Neptune does. So some astronomers thought it might once have been a satellite of Neptune that got knocked away in some cosmic catastrophe. But they have traced its orbit back in time, and it doesn't seem that it was ever close enough to Neptune to have been its satellite.

Right: Pluto's orbit takes the planet far from the plane in which the other planets orbit. At its closest to the Sun, Pluto is actually closer than Neptune.

Opposite: Is Pluto an escaped moon of Neptune? It's an interesting thought, but scientists are doubtful that Pluto ever orbited Neptune.

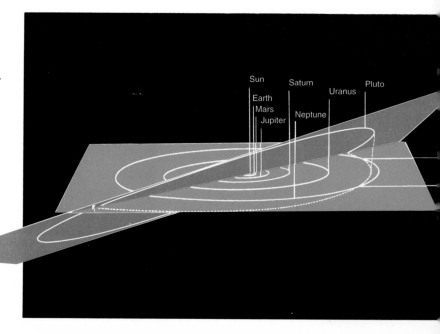

Companion Charon

Between 1979 and 1999, Pluto is closer to the Sun than Neptune is. Pluto can also be seen better at this time than at any other time.

In 1978, astronomer James W. Christy noticed a bulge on a photograph he had taken of Pluto. He looked at earlier photos and found the bulge in different spots. Christy discovered that Pluto has a moon moving around it. He named the moon Charon (pronounced *Sharon*) after his wife Char. By coincidence, in Greek mythology, the boatman who transported spirits to the underworld – the realm of the god Pluto – is also named Charon (pronounced *KAIR-on*).

Charon is about half as wide as Pluto. No other known planet has a satellite that similar to it in size. This means that Pluto is practically a double planet. Only Earth and its Moon, which is about one quarter the width of Earth, come that close to being a double planet.

Opposite: An artist's view of Pluto and Charon forming from the rocky debris at the edge of the Solar System – one idea of how they formed.

Below, top: This picture showed astronomer James Christy that Pluto has a moon. The bulge *(right)* appears in different places in other pictures.

Below, bottom: Charon, boatman of the Greek underworld.

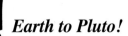

Earth to Pluto!

Most moons are much smaller than their parent planets. Ganymede has only 1/12,000 the mass of Jupiter. Titan has just 1/4,000 of Saturn's mass. Our Moon, however, has 1/80 the mass of Earth. For ages, Earth-Moon was the closest thing to a double planet in our Solar System. But then came Charon, which is about 1/8 the mass of Pluto. Pluto and Charon are much smaller than Earth and its Moon, but they are a great deal closer to being a double planet.

? The origins of Charon – a chip off the old block?

Why should Pluto have so large a moon? Giant planets sometimes capture small objects that wander too closely to them. But Pluto is far too small to capture anything the size of Charon. Pluto and Charon may once have been a single body that somehow broke apart. That would explain why they are separated by only 12,400 miles (19,950 km) – 1/20 the distance between Earth and the Moon. But what would have caused the original planet to break up? Scientists do not know.

Small Worlds After All

When astronomers first searched for Pluto, they thought it must be fairly large to pull sufficiently at Neptune and Uranus. But Pluto was much smaller than they had expected. In addition, the newly discovered planet was much dimmer than they had expected.

On June 9, 1988, Pluto moved in front of a star. Based on the time that the star remained hidden, astronomers calculated that Pluto was 1,457 miles (2,344 km) across – smaller than Earth's Moon. In fact, Pluto weighs only about one-fifth as much as our Moon, and Charon weighs only one-fifth as much as Pluto. Pluto and Charon are very small worlds indeed.

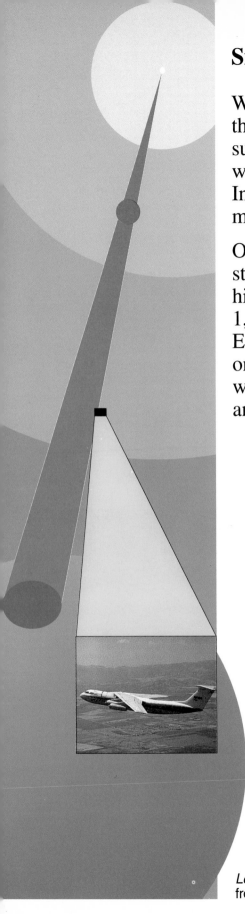

Opposite, top: Charon may have formed from the cloud of debris created when an asteroid or comet collided with Pluto long ago.

Opposite, bottom: Earth is eighty times more massive than the Moon *(top scale).* Pluto is just eight times more massive than its moon, Charon *(bottom scale).*

Left: When Pluto passed in front of a star, astronomers got a chance to search for a thin atmosphere around the planet. While Pluto was in front of the star, sensitive instruments searched the star's light for any changes caused by gases surrounding Pluto.

Inset: Astronomers aboard NASA's Kuiper Airborne Observatory, a telescope-equipped jet plane, were the first to detect Pluto's thin atmosphere.

Uncovering Pluto

Despite its small size and great distance from Earth, astronomers have managed to discover some details about Pluto.

In the 1950s, astronomers found that Pluto's light grew slightly dimmer and then slightly brighter every 6.4 days. They realized this was because Pluto turned on its axis in that time, showing a brighter side and a dimmer side as it turned.

Then, in 1976, by analyzing light reflected from Pluto, astronomers showed that it was covered with frozen methane, a chemical found in natural gas on Earth. They also found that Pluto is lighter at its poles and darker at its equator.

Opposite: On Earth, pockets of methane accompany oil deep underground. Here, an oil refinery burns off excess methane.

Below: When it's summertime on Pluto, the planet's thin layer of frozen methane turns into a gas and creates an atmosphere. Darker material beneath the ice then becomes visible, and Pluto appears dimmer *(left).* During winter, the gases in the atmosphere freeze and brighten Pluto with a fresh coat of methane snow *(right).*

Sharing the "Air"

When Pluto's orbit brings it nearest Earth, Charon moves in front of it and then behind it every 6.4 days.

By studying the light of Pluto when Charon is hidden behind it, and by studying both bodies when Charon is in front, astronomers have found that Charon is darker than Pluto.

Pluto is big enough and cold enough – from -350° Fahrenheit (-212°Centigrade) down to -390°F (-234°C) – to have a thin atmosphere of methane gas. Charon is just as cold, although it is smaller and has less gravity. But Charon has lost its methane and is composed of ice made from water.

Pluto and Charon are so close in distance and in size that particles in Pluto's atmosphere extend to Charon. These form a thin methane cloud over the entire Pluto-Charon system. So Pluto-Charon is a double planet enclosed in a single atmosphere.

Opposite: If you were standing on Charon during one of its eclipses of Pluto, you could watch the dark shadow of Charon sweep across the frozen surface of Pluto.

Below: When Charon passes in front of Pluto, astronomers call it an "inferior eclipse." When the shadow of Pluto falls on Charon, it is called a "superior eclipse."

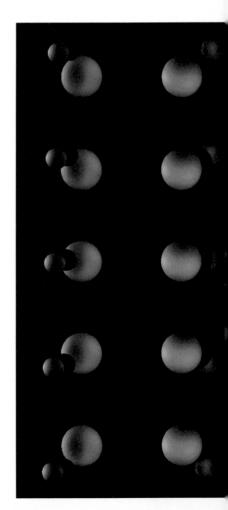

❗ *Pluto and Charon – a cosmic face-off!*

When a small celestial body circles a larger one, its rotation is slowed by tides. This is why a moon faces only one side to its planet – its speed of rotation has been slowed down. Earth's Moon faces only one side to

Earth. The larger planet also slows, but it is so massive, it slows just slightly. Only in the case of Pluto and Charon are the two bodies so small and so nearly equal in size that each faces the same side to the other.

Starry Days and Nights

Pluto is so far from the Sun, that from Pluto's surface, the Sun looks quite different than it does from Earth. Viewing the Sun from Pluto, you might think of the Sun as just another star. Even when Pluto is at its closest to the Sun, it gets only about 1/900 as much sunlight as Earth gets. No wonder Pluto is so cold.

Still, from remote Pluto, the Sun looks a thousand times brighter than the full Moon looks when viewed from Earth. Because Pluto's thin atmosphere does not scatter sunlight the way Earth's atmosphere does, stars are visible from Pluto even with the Sun in the sky.

From Pluto, the Sun is still fourteen million times brighter than any other star. After all, the next nearest star is thousands of times farther away than the Sun.

Left: Ice crystals in Pluto's atmosphere create a rare arc of light around the distant Sun. It's the beginning of Pluto's long winter, and methane snow has started to coat the planet's surface as the atmosphere freezes.

21

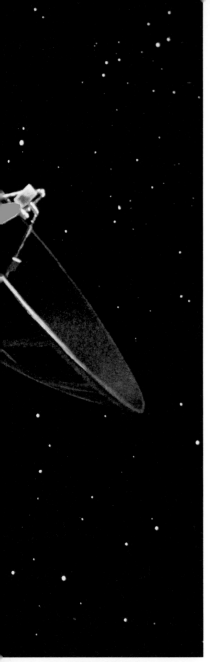

Pluto Fast Flyby

So far, spacecraft have explored all the planets except one – Pluto. One scientist calls Pluto the "Mount Everest" of Solar System exploration because it is the most distant, coldest, and hardest planet to reach.

NASA is designing a mission to send two small spacecraft to Pluto and Charon. The two probes will take pictures and gather data about the mysterious Pluto and Charon. The mission is called the "Pluto Fast Flyby."

In the meantime, the Hubble Space Telescope is taking excellent pictures of Pluto and its companion. Scientists are combining new data with what they already know to complete the picture of Pluto and Charon.

Top: Astronomers hope that a Pluto Fast Flyby mission will complete our first tour of the Solar System. Pluto is the only planet that has not been visited by spacecraft from Earth.

Opposite, bottom, left: Astronomers have studied observations of Pluto and put together these computer maps of the light and dark markings of the planet.

Opposite, bottom, right and immediate left: These pictures of Pluto and Charon were taken by the Hubble Space Telescope. The picture on the *immediate left* was taken before the telescope was repaired. A sharper view is seen *(opposite)* after repairs were made to the orbiting observatory in 1993.

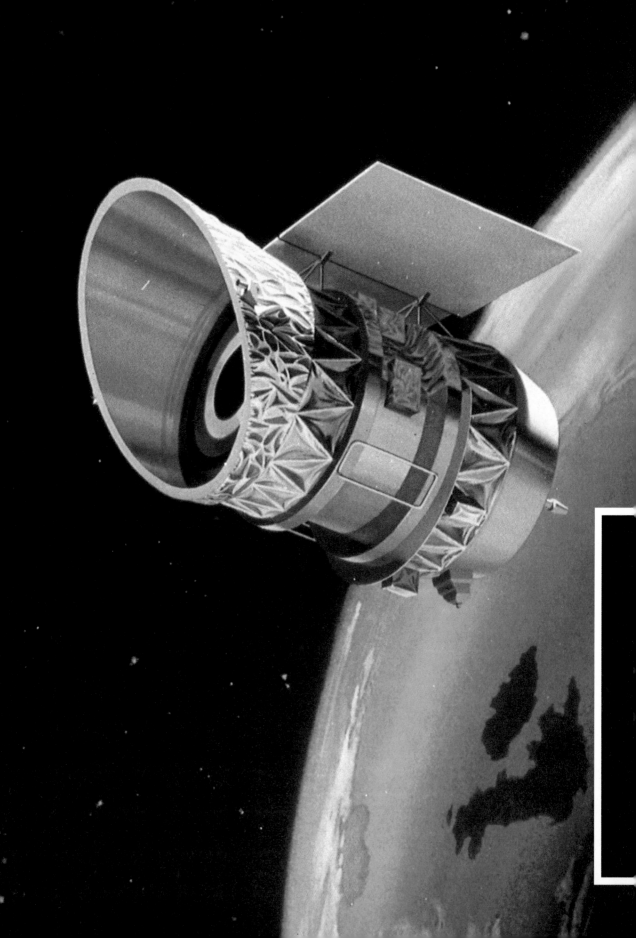

A Tenth Planet?

Pluto was found in a search for a planet whose gravity was tugging at Uranus and Neptune. However, scientists now know that Pluto's gravity is too weak to make any difference at all. For that reason, many people have searched for a tenth planet beyond Pluto. Such a planet would have to have enough gravity to make Uranus and Neptune follow their slightly wobbly orbits. Recently, though, some astronomers have decided that Uranus and Neptune do not really wobble after all. They believe early observations of these planets are not reliable. The proof lies in the fact that spacecraft have successfully been sent to Uranus and Neptune using calculations that were not based on the early observations.

Left: The Infrared Astronomical Satellite (IRAS), a telescope sensitive to heat, has searched the entire sky for objects too cool to glow by their own light – such as a tenth planet – and none was found. *Inset:* An infrared map of the sky. The bright band is the Milky Way.

Below: This device is a special camera designed to look for faint objects beyond Neptune. It has been used to find many small objects in space, but no tenth planet or large "Planet X."

Is Pluto Really a Planet?

Because of Pluto's small size and lopsided orbit, many people have wondered whether Pluto should be considered a planet at all. Other celestial objects, like the asteroid Chiron, have orbits similar to Pluto's. Plus, seven moons of other planets are larger than Pluto! Some people have said that, since Pluto has a moon, it must be a planet. But astronomers recently discovered that the asteroid Ida has a moon. Other asteroids and comets probably do, too.

An important recent discovery is the Kuiper Belt of objects orbiting beyond Neptune. Many astronomers think Pluto is just one of the largest of the thousands of these objects. They believe Neptune is the last "real" planet.

We still have much to learn about Pluto – the most distant member of our Solar System!

Opposite: In the twenty-second century, humans may view Pluto and Charon in person, as interplanetary visitors.
Inset: A comet in orbit far from the Sun in a collection of comets called the Oort Cloud. Just like planets, comets may also have moons.

Below, left: Pluto has an odd orbit like the recently discovered asteroids in the Kuiper Belt. More and more of these objects are being found all the time. Perhaps a new "Pluto" will be among them.

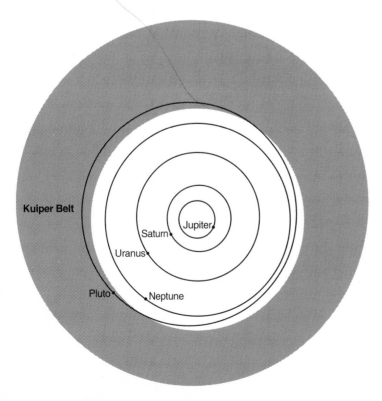

Fact File: Pluto's Secrets Revealed

Pluto, our Solar System's smallest known planet, is also the farthest from the Sun. It takes the longest of any known planet to orbit the Sun – nearly 248 Earth years.

Tiny Pluto is still revealing many of its secrets to astronomers. One of Pluto's most exciting aspects – the existence of its moon, Charon – came to light in 1978.

Charon is very close to its companion planet in size, mass, and distance. Pluto and Charon seem to be a double planet. Astronomers now believe that Charon and Pluto may even share the same atmosphere.

Three other planets – Jupiter, Saturn, and Earth – have moons that are bigger than the planet Pluto. In the minds of some astronomers, without its moon and atmosphere, tiny Pluto barely qualifies as a planet at all!

Above: The Sun and its Solar System family, *left to right:* Mercury, Venus, Earth, Mars, Jupiter, Saturn, Uranus, Neptune, and Pluto. *Inset:* Pluto *(far right)* and its moon, Charon *(immediate right).*

Pluto's Moon

Name	Diameter	Distance From Pluto's Center
Charon	745 miles (1,200 km)	12,700 miles (20,450 km)

Pluto: How It Measures Up to Earth

Planet	Diameter	Rotation Period (length of day)	Moons	Period of Orbit around Sun (length of year)	Surface Gravity	Distance from Sun (nearest-farthest)	Least Time It Takes Light to Travel to Earth
Pluto	1,457 miles (2,344 km)	6 days, 9 hours, 18 minutes	1	247.7 years	0.06*	2.7-4.6 billion miles (4.4-7.4 billion km)	3.9 hours
Earth	7,927 miles (12,756 km)	23 hours, 56 minutes	1	365.25 days	1.00*	91-94.5 million miles (147-152 million km)	—

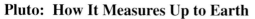

* Multiply your weight by this number to find out how much you would weigh on this planet.

More Books about Pluto

Discovery of Pluto. Tombaugh (Astronomical Society of the Pacific)
Exploring Outer Space: Rockets, Probes, and Satellites. Asimov (Gareth Stevens)
Our Planetary System. Asimov (Gareth Stevens)
The Planet Pluto. Whyte (Pergamon)
The Planets. Couper (Franklin Watts)
Whitney's Star Finder. Whitney (Knopf)

Videos

Our Solar System. (Gareth Stevens)
Pluto: A Double Planet? (Gareth Stevens)

Places to Visit

You can explore Pluto and other parts of the Universe without leaving Earth. Here are some museums and centers where you can find a variety of space exhibits.

International Women's
    Air and Space Museum
1 Chamber Plaza
Dayton, OH 45402

NASA Lewis Research Center
Educational Services Office
21000 Brookpark Road
Cleveland, OH 44135

Edmonton Space and Science Centre
11211 - 142nd Street
Edmonton, Alberta K5M 4A1

Henry Crown Science Center
Museum of Science and Industry
57th Street and Lake Shore Drive
Chicago, IL 60637

Perth Observatory
Walnut Road
Bickley, W.A. 6076
Australia

Seneca College Planetarium
1750 Finch Avenue East
North York, Ontario M2J 2X5

Places to Write

Here are some places you can write for more information about Pluto. Be sure to state what kind of information you would like. Include your full name and address for a reply.

Jet Propulsion Laboratory
Teacher Resource Center
4800 Oak Grove Drive
Pasadena, CA 91109

Canadian Space Agency
Communications Department
6767 Route de L'Aeroport
Saint Hubert, Quebec J3Y 8Y9

National Space Science Data Center
NASA Goddard Space Flight Center
Greenbelt Road - Code 633 - Building 26
Greenbelt, MD 20771

Sydney Observatory
P.O. Box K346
Haymarket 2000 Australia

Glossary

astronomer: a person who observes and studies the Universe and its various celestial bodies.

atmosphere: the gases that surround a planet, star, or moon.

axis: the imaginary straight line around which a planet, star, or moon turns.

billion: the number represented by 1 followed by nine zeroes – 1,000,000,000. In some countries, this number is called "a thousand million." In these countries, one billion would then be represented by 1 followed by twelve zeroes – 1,000,000,000,000 – a million million.

comet: an object in space made of ice, rock, and gas. It has a vapor tail that can be seen from Earth when the comet's orbit brings it close to the Sun.

double planet: planets that circle each other.

eclipse: the partial or complete blocking of light from one astronomical body by another.

elliptical: oval in shape.

equator: the imaginary line around the middle of a planet that is always an equal distance from the two poles of the planet. The equator divides the planet into two half-spheres, or hemispheres.

gravity: the force that causes objects like Earth and the Moon to be drawn toward one another.

Kuiper Belt: a grouping of objects, such as asteroids, orbiting the Solar System beyond Neptune.

methane gas: a colorless, odorless, flammable gas.

observatory: a building or other structure designed for watching and recording celestial objects and events.

Oort Cloud: a grouping of comets surrounding the Solar System, named after Jan Oort, the Dutch astronomer who suggested its existence in 1950.

orbit: the path that one celestial object follows as it circles, or revolves, around another.

pole: either end of the axis around which a planet, moon, or star rotates.

probe: a craft that travels in space, photographing and studying celestial bodies and even landing on some of them.

satellite: a smaller body that orbits a larger body. The Moon is Earth's natural satellite. *Sputnik 1* and *2* were Earth's first artificial satellites.

Solar System: our Sun with the planets and all other celestial bodies, such as asteroids, that orbit the Sun.

Sun: Earth's star and the provider of the energy that makes life possible on Earth.

underworld: in Greek mythology, the place where it was believed people went when they died.

Index

Born in 1920, Isaac Asimov came to the United States as a young boy from his native Russia. As a young man, he was a student of biochemistry. In time, he became one of the most productive writers the world has ever known. His books cover a spectrum of topics, including science, history, language theory, fantasy, and science fiction. His brilliant imagination gained him the respect and admiration of adults and children alike. Sadly, Isaac Asimov died shortly after the publication of the first edition of *Isaac Asimov's Library of the Universe.*

The publishers wish to thank the following for permission to reproduce copyright material: front cover, © Paul Dimare 1989; 4, copyright-free reproduction from Heck, J. G., *The Complete Encyclopedia of Illustration*; 5, © Rick Karpinski/DeWalt and Associates 1989; 6, © Keith Ward 1989; 7 (all), Lowell Observatory; 8-9, © Lynette Cook 1989; 9, © Julian Baum 1989; 10-11, © Sally Bensusen 1982; 11, © Paul Dimare 1989; 12 (upper), U. S. Navy; 12 (lower), © Keith Ward 1989; 13, 14 (upper), © Michael Carroll 1989; 14 (lower), © Lynette Cook 1989; 15 (large), Kate Kriege/© Gareth Stevens, Inc.; 15 (inset), NASA; 16 (both), © Paul Dimare 1989; 17, © Stewart M. Green, Tom Stack and Associates; 18, Marc W. Buie, Space Telescope Science Institute; 19, © Joe Shabram 1987; 20-21, © John Foster 1985; 22 (left), © Walter J. Wild, University of Chicago; 22 (right), Dr. R. Albrecht, ESA/ESO Space Telescope European Coordinating Facility, and NASA; 22-23; © Michael Carroll; 23, European Space Agency; 24-25 (both), Jet Propulsion Laboratory; 25, Courtesy Gerard Luppino, Institute for Astronomy, University of Hawaii; 26, © Gareth Stevens, Inc.; 26-27, © Michael Carroll; 27, © Pat Rawlings 1989; 28-29, © Sally Bensusen 1987; 29, © Sally Bensusen 1989.